MW01170741

Maxims of Leadership
Coaching the Uncoachable

Michael Gatewood

ISBN:978-0-9844678-5-3

DEDICATION

This book is dedicated to the men, women, and youth who empowered and helped me developed my soft skills.

CONTENTS

ACKNOWLEDGMENTS

Mr. Torres Bennett, thank you for your open door and always willing to make things right. Ms. Harvey, a great teacher and mentor, wish you could have taught me more. Mr. Anthony Nottingham taught me it's not just about getting things done, it's how. Bo Daniels "Stay out of the way and God will make your way" Mr. Justino Rodriguez always takes time to teach and make sure you understand. Ms. Brenda J. Cleveland showed me the ropes to give the youth hope. Mr. Rufus Brown who taught me to be a man of the people. The cleaning lady lol, Ms. Robin Berry, COO that's how she introduced herself. Fortunately, she hired some bright employees who realized the position didn't suit her disposition. Mr. Janus Pierre for always pushing me to be better. Mr. Rob was always willing to give advice when I didn't have a clue. Mr. Mike Akers for support and inspiration even when I didn't know I needed it. Mr. Anthony Brathwaite who taught me "When they go high you stay low" Facility Administrator Mr. Wilson who fought to give me an opportunity which is what I do for the youth and staff.

PART I THE ER

ER - The emergency room, the place where employees await "employee recognition" the place, where they are looking to be recognized and not criticized. The place where they are in the spotlight! The place where you highlight their abilities and not inadequacies! The place where the experienced become experts, because of expectations, without speculation, and or frustration. The place where people work with you is not just for you.

ER | Employee Recognition Part I

"Admonition is not Ammunition"- GEM:
Navigating the Terrain of Constructive Criticism

Introduction

In a world quick to judge and slow to understand, the maxim "Admonition is not Ammunition" presents a timely reflection on the nature of criticism and the art of giving and receiving feedback. The phrase suggests that corrective feedback—admonition—is not meant to be a weapon in interpersonal conflicts but a tool for growth and improvement.

The Power of Words: A Double-Edged Sword:

The words we speak carry immense power. They have the potential to build individuals up or tear them down. When used thoughtlessly, words can become ammunition, inflicting wounds that fester and scar. However, words can also act as medicine, able to heal and encourage when delivered with care and compassion.

Admonition: A Constructive Force

Admonition, at its core, is about guidance rather than chastisement. It involves pointing out mistakes or poor behavior not to condemn but to enlighten and assist someone in their journey of self-improvement. This distinction is critical, for it is the intent behind the admonition that determines whether the outcome is positive or detrimental.

Constructive criticism is an art form steeped in emotional intelligence. It requires the critic to empathize with the recipient, to put themselves in the other person's shoes, and to deliver feedback with a blend of honesty and sensitivity. Admonition of this nature is supportive; it nurtures growth and fosters a positive environment where individuals are encouraged to learn from their mistakes.

Ammunition: The Fallacy of Forceful Criticism

The concept of using criticism as ammunition is predicated on the notion that forceful, harsh feedback is the best way to incite change. However, this approach often backfires, as it can put the recipient on the defensive, shutting down communication and hindering progress. When feedback is weaponized, it loses its constructive value and becomes merely an outlet for frustration or a display of power.

The Balancing Act: Delivering Effective Feedback

Striking the right balance when giving admonition is instrumental in ensuring that the message is well received. The technique commonly referred to as the "sandwich method"—where constructive criticism is nestled between two positive statements—serves as a practical approach that tempers the sting of critique. The recipient feels acknowledged and valued, which can lead to a more open-minded reception of the feedback.

Furthermore, the context in which feedback is provided is as important as the feedback itself. Delivery in a private setting, paced thoughtfully, and with a focus on specific behaviors rather than personal traits, equips individuals with actionable insights rather than leaving them feeling attacked.

Conclusion: Embracing the True Spirit of Admonition

The maxim "Admonition is not Ammunition" champions the ethos of constructive feedback. It serves as a reminder that the ultimate goal of critique is not to diminish but to develop. As we engage with others in our personal and professional lives, let us embrace the spirit of this maxim—using our words to guide, to help, and to heal.

By fostering a culture where admonition is seen as a valuable tool for personal and collective growth, we contribute to a more empathetic and understanding society. Whether we are on the giving or receiving end of feedback, acknowledging that admonition is designed to construct rather than destruct can enrich our interactions and help forge stronger, more respectful relationships.

ER | Employee Recognition Part Il

"No Condemnation Just Approbation"-
GEM: Shifting from Critique to Praise in Personal Growth

Introduction

Rejecting the punitive impulse to condemn and embracing the supportive instinct to approve is a paradigm encapsulated by the phrase "No Condemnation Just Approbation." This maxim reflects an attitude towards personal and professional development that prioritizes encouragement over censure.

Understanding Condemnation and its Consequences

Condemnation implies strong disapproval and can often lead to a form of social or emotional sentencing. It is punitive and reflects a finality—a judgment passed that leaves little room for redemption. This harsh approach can cripple an individual's self-esteem, stifle creativity, and engender a climate of fear rather than motivation.

Those who face condemnation may become wary of taking risks or trying new approaches for fear of further rebuke. In an environment where failure is not tolerated, growth is often stunted, and the potential for innovation is quashed by the heavy weight of potential criticism.

The Psychology Behind Approbation

Approbation, on the contrary, is an affirmation of something positive. It is a warm endorsement that fosters an individual's sense of worth and validates their efforts. Demonstrating approbation can inspire one to strive harder, secure in the knowledge that their contributions are valued and that their growth is supported.

Positive reinforcement, a key tenet of behavioral psychology, suggests that behaviors followed by positive stimuli are more likely to be repeated. In this way, approbation serves as a vital tool in encouraging constructive behaviors and personal development.

Creating a Culture of Positive Recognition

Establishing a culture of positive recognition, where approbation is the norm, requires a shift in perspective. It involves focusing on strengths rather than solely identifying weaknesses. While not ignoring areas that require improvement, this approach balances critique with a heavy dose of praise for achievements and effort.

In practice, this culture rewards the process as much as the outcome, acknowledging that effort, perseverance, and resilience are worth celebrating, even if they do not always yield perfect results. It's recognition that progress, not just perfection, is deserving of accolades.

The Art of Constructive Feedback

While the maxim suggests an emphasis on approbation over condemnation, it does not advocate for the elimination of constructive criticism. The key lies in ensuring that feedback is framed in a supportive context. For instance, employing a strengths-based approach can help individuals capitalize on what they do well, while simultaneously addressing areas of improvement.

In such a setting, individuals are equipped to receive feedback as a means to further develop their abilities rather than as a discouraging reprimand. This nuanced understanding of feedback, where constructive dialogue is prioritized, can foster a more dynamic and empowering environment.

Conclusion: The Paradigm of Positive Growth

The maxim "No Condemnation Just Approbation" suggests a fundamental shift in how we perceive and enact personal growth. It calls for an environment where encouragement and positive reinforcement are the prevailing winds, guiding individuals toward their potential.

By focusing on what people are doing right and offering supportive guidance for improvement, we not only enrich their individual experiences but also contribute to a more compassionate and constructive community. It is this focus on the affirmative, on building rather than dismantling, that can propel individuals and societies toward a brighter, more nurturing future.

ER | Employee Recognition Part III

The phrase *"Criticism and sarcasm isn't necessary for activism" - GEM* underlines the principle that promoting change and championing causes do not require negativity or derision to be effective. Here's an exploration of this concept:

Positive Activism: Beyond Criticism and Sarcasm

Introduction

Activism—advocating for change and challenging the status quo—has traditionally been associated with vociferous criticism and sharp sarcasm aimed at drawing attention to social injustices. However, the assertion "Criticism and sarcasm isn't necessary for activism" suggests a different model of social engagement, one that relies on positivity, constructive dialogue, and solution-oriented approaches.

The Limitations of Negative Tactics

While criticism and sarcasm can be effective tools for drawing attention to issues, their overuse can sometimes result in alienating the very people activists seek to persuade. Sarcasm, in particular, can be misinterpreted as condescension, undermining the message and breeding resentment rather than fostering understanding and cooperation.

Criticism, when not paired with constructive alternatives, runs the risk of creating a narrative of opposition without offering a path forward. This can lead to polarized discussions where the focus is on what is wrong rather than how things can be improved.

Positive Activism: A Constructive Alternative

Positive activism focuses on what can be done to create change rather than what is going wrong. It is rooted in empathy, understanding, and collaboration. This form of activism amplifies hope and the belief that change is possible through collective action and constructive engagement.

Advocates of positive activism use education, peaceful demonstration, and the promotion of alternatives to inspire rather than incite, to uplift rather than degrade. They empower communities by highlighting strengths and resources that can be harnessed for progress.

Inclusivity and Dialogue

An important aspect of positive activism is the inclusion of diverse voices and perspectives. This approach values dialogue over diatribe and seeks to build bridges rather than barriers. It aims to engage opponents in meaningful conversation, finding common ground and shared values as a starting point for change.

Through respectful dialogue, activists can foster a greater understanding of the complexities of an issue, enlisting allies across different spheres of society. Inclusion breeds commitment, as people are more likely to support changes they have been involved in shaping.

Celebrating Successes

Positive activists are keen to celebrate small victories along the way to larger goals. Recognizing progress—no matter how incremental—serves as a motivational force and validates the efforts of those involved. It's a way of building momentum and sustaining energy for the long-term work that activism often entails.

The Role of Imagination

Instead of wielding criticism and sarcasm, positive activism invites creative thought. Imagining new possibilities and innovative solutions is central to effecting change. By using positive messaging and highlighting what could be, activists can paint a compelling picture of the future that draws people together behind a shared vision.

Conclusion: A Call for Hope and Humanity

"Criticism and sarcasm aren't necessary for activism" is a call for a more compassionate and constructive form of social engagement. It is a recognition that how we advocate for change is as important as the change itself. By cultivating hope, inclusivity, and celebrating successes, positive activism offers a holistic approach that nurtures the spirit of community and fosters sustainable change.

Positive activism reaffirms that we need not tear down to build up and that a brighter future isn't achieved through negativity but through the relentless pursuit of progress with a heart full of hope and humanity.

PART II SL| SERVANT LEADERSHIP

Matthew 23:11 CEV

"Whoever is the greatest should be the servant of the others"

"Servant leaders strongly believe that they have a duty of stewardship. They are people-centric and value services to others in general and more specifically to their followers. In organizational settings, servant leaders believe in every employee and treat them with respect and humility. The employee is given an opportunity to do meaningful work. Favorable attitudes of employees toward their supervisors were found to be related to the productivity of employees."
-Forbes Magazine

SL I | *"People who can't relate retaliate."*
-GEM

"People don't care how much you know they want to know how much you care." -Theodore Rosevelt

Individuals who feel misunderstood or disconnected often manifest their frustrations through acts of retaliation.

The sentiment captured by Theodore Roosevelt -- that people value empathy over expertise -- speaks volumes about human relationships. The question to ponder is whether you prioritize being comprehended. Consider whether your phone is brimming with contacts, yet you find yourself devoid of any profound or genuine connections. There's a notable pattern where leaders who deliberately keep a professional distance from their team members may inadvertently prompt an emotional disconnect. Such detachment can lead to team members seeking to sever ties, driven by the fundamental human need for recognition and empathy. In the workplace, the desire for esteem can be gendered; men often prize honor and respect, whereas women are more likely to appreciate emotional insight and connection.

"Leaders who avoid closeness with subordinates often end up with subordinates desiring closure."

The act of truly listening to someone cannot be overstated. When people feel ignored or dismissed, their reaction can often be one of antagonism, projecting their hurt onto others. True leadership involves empathizing with the motivations of your team to realize the collective expectations.

To effectively lead with a relational approach, there are quintessential elements to grasp. These include:

1. Inclusion: Fostering an environment where everyone feels seen, heard, and valued.
2. Empowerment: Giving team members the authority and confidence to take initiative and make decisions.
3. Purposefulness: Leading with intention and clarity, ensuring that all team members understand the vision and their role in achieving it.
4. Ethical Behaviors: Upholding moral standards and leading by example to engender trust and respect.
5. Process Orientation: Paying attention to the processes that guide the daily actions and interactions within the team, not just the outcomes.

Integrating these facets into your leadership style can radically transform the dynamics of your team.

It not only creates a more cohesive and supportive work environment but also aligns individual aspirations with the collective mission. Leaders who master the art of relational leadership are not just commanders; they are architects of a community within their organization, cultivating a culture where every member thrives and contributes effectively to the greater goal. Remember, until you can feel a person's motivation you can't fulfill your expectation!

SL ll | *"Don't take it personal but Do be personal-able"- GEM*

Understanding the Art of Being Approachable Without Being Overly Sensitive

Mastering the art of personable leadership involves cultivating the skill of engaging with others authentically and warmly while not letting personal feelings get in the way of professional interactions. The essence of being approachable lies in your ability to create a personal bond, making people feel heard and understood, especially under the pressure of stressful circumstances. This brand of leadership is all about empowering relationships through emotional strength and empathy.

To kickstart genuine personal connections, begin by engaging in social interactions. Extend sincere compliments to acknowledge the efforts and accomplishments of others. Offer a comforting word or gesture to someone in need, express your vulnerabilities in a measured way to show your humanity, and regularly share your gratitude to foster a positive environment. Quick and effective ways to establish rapport include maintaining direct eye contact, which conveys your full attention and interest; asking thoughtful questions to show that you value their input; adopting open body language to demonstrate your openness to the conversation; retaining an optimistic demeanor to instill confidence and positivity; and practicing active listening to ensure that you're fully engaged with the person you are speaking to.

Being 'personal-able' means that you balance your openness with a level of professionalism that guards you against taking things too personal. It's crucial to remember that the moment you start to internalize external feedback or issues, your capacity to lead and manage personnel could be affected. It's about being present and empathetic, without letting your emotions dictate your leadership style. By drawing this line, you will be able to support your team effectively while maintaining your professional integrity. Remember, the strongest leaders are those who can connect with their team on a human level while staying resilient in the face of personal challenges. Being personal-able doesn't give you the right to take things personally. Remember anything you take personally will affect how you lead personnel! Also, anything you take personally reflects how staff respond to you professionally.

SL III| *"Be responsible to people not for people"- GEM*

Your responsibility is to people not for people. Often in leadership, we are responsible for leading the people, we are not responsible for people's feelings about or towards your leadership. I'm not saying not to care about your team, I'm saying don't carry their feelings on your back that you can't be effective. You can care for the team without carrying their Ill feelings towards you or your leadership.

As a leader, your primary obligation is to serve the people you lead by providing direction, support, and vision. This responsibility is more about enabling your team to excel and less about taking personal responsibility for each individual's emotions or reactions to your leadership approach. Effective leadership requires a clear understanding of this distinction.

Leadership is not about controlling or manipulating emotions but rather about inspiring and empowering individuals to reach their potential. While it is natural for leaders to be concerned with their team's morale, it's important to recognize that you cannot—and should not—attempt to manage every aspect of their emotional response to your decisions or style of leadership. Your role is to steer the team towards common goals, not to bear the weight of their personal feelings about the way you lead.

Empathy is an essential trait for any leader. Sensitivity to the needs and feelings of your team can help create a supportive and positive work environment. However, there is a fine balance to maintain. Being overly preoccupied with how your team feels about you can be counterproductive, as it may distract you from making objective, strategic decisions that are in the best interest of the project or organization.

It is possible to be considerate and understanding without taking personal responsibility for your team's grievances or dissatisfaction with leadership. Providing a space for open communication, encouraging feedback, and addressing concerns can all be done without internalizing the negativity that might arise. The focus should remain on collaborative problem-solving and fostering a resilient team dynamic.

By maintaining professional boundaries and focusing on what you can control—like the direction and values of your organization—you can guide your team effectively while also promoting a separation between the roles of leadership and personal emotional responsibility. Your effectiveness as a leader is not measured by how much emotional weight you carry for your team but by how well you can navigate them through challenges and toward success.

SL IV| The Perils of Favoritism in Leadership

In the realm of leadership and governance, a timeless principle reverberates through the halls of decision-making and public service: *"**Favor the people, not the person"**. - **GEM**** This axiom holds a wealth of wisdom within its concise message, reminding those in power that the collective well-being of the community should supersede individual interests. Moreover, it carries an implicit cautionary tale—that favoritism can backfire, ultimately leading to dishonor and disrepute.

At its core, this principal advocate for an egalitarian approach to leadership. When the needs of the people—a diverse and vast collective—are prioritized, the foundation for a just and fair society is laid. Favoritism, on the other hand, can create an environment ripe with corruption, nepotism, and discord. It breeds resentment among those who perceive themselves as less favored and undermines the trust that is essential for any leader or public figure to effectively govern or influence.

The saying "Favorites require favors" captures the transactional nature of favoritism that further erodes the integrity of a fair and impartial system. In such scenarios, favoritism is not without cost; the individual who is favored may be expected to repay the preferential treatment they receive. This cycle of reciprocal favors disrupts the balance of a meritocratic system where opportunities and rewards are meant to be based on individual merit and not personal relationships or biases.

History and contemporary events are replete with cautionary examples where leaders who have honored an individual above the collective have faced the wrath of the masses. The people, once feeling ignored or marginalized in favor of a select few, can retract their support and respect for the leader. This backlash can manifest as public protests, a decline in the leader's approval ratings, or more severe political repercussions.

It is, therefore, not only a matter of ethical governance but also of pragmatic leadership to avoid favoritism and instead, nurture a culture of equity and fairness. Leaders who acknowledge the diversity of their constituents and strive to meet the needs of their population gain honor and trust. They send a clear message that each person, irrespective of their status or connections, is valued and will be treated with the same consideration.

In conclusion, the stark reminder embedded in the adage nudges leaders at every level to reflect on their actions and policies through the lens of collective benefit. To honor one person above the people is to risk the very foundation of one's leadership. True honor, and indeed the longevity of respect and power, emanates from a leader's unwavering commitment to the people they serve. It is a lesson in humility and responsibility, demanding that leaders consistently align their actions with the greater good to maintain the honor and dignity vested in them by the very people they represent.

If you honor one person above the people, the people will dishonor you because of the person.

SL V | The Power of a Question

The maxim ***"The answer isn't qualified until you qualify it with a question"-GEM***, when leaders refuse to answer questions, their actions seem questionable! reflects the critical importance of transparency, curiosity, and open dialogue ineffective leadership. It suggests that answers only gain legitimacy when they are in response to well-considered questions, implying a process of inquiry and challenge that's fundamental to understanding and legitimacy.

Let's unpack this statement:

Qualifying Answers with Questions:

- In organizations, answers provided by leaders or managers need to be rooted in a clear understanding of the issues at hand. This is achieved through questions that clarify, probe, and challenge. Asking the right questions can illuminate underlying assumptions, reveal additional information, and lead to more nuanced and informed outcomes. It ensures that answers are tailored to the actual complexities of the situation rather than being based on surface-level understanding.

Leadership Transparency:

- When leaders are open to questioning, it demonstrates their confidence in their decisions and their willingness to engage in constructive dialogue. It also indicates a level of transparency and accountability, which are cornerstones of trust within an organization.

Actions Under Scrutiny:

- Leaders who reject questions or avoid providing answers can fuel doubt about the integrity and validity of their actions. If leadership seems averse to scrutiny, it may cast a shadow on their decision-making processes, leading to speculation, mistrust, and a perceived lack of authenticity or ethical standards.

Building Trust: - Conversely, when leaders can justify their actions with clear, honest responses to probing questions, they build trust with their teams. This trust is essential for maintaining morale, aligning the team with the organization's mission, and driving collective action toward shared goals.

Incorporating this principle into leadership behavior means fostering an environment where questioning is encouraged and responded to with thoughtful, substantive answers. Such an environment promotes a culture of continuous learning and active engagement, wherein:

- Team members feel valued and that their concerns and curiosities are legitimate.
- Leaders are seen as accessible and open to dialog, reinforcing their role as guides and facilitators.
- Decision-making processes are more likely to be incremental and collaborative, which can enhance the quality and outcomes of those decisions.

Ultimately, this approach not only keeps leadership actions above reproach but also underlines the value of intellectual exchange and critical thinking in forging a strong and resilient organization.

SL VI| *"Better an Apology instead of a Eulogy" -GEM*

The phrase "Better an Apology instead of a Eulogy" paired with the sentiment "Don't take it personally but be personable" offers profound guidance for personal and professional interactions. It alludes to the value of recognizing and addressing one's own mistakes promptly, with humility and sincerity, rather than allowing situations to deteriorate to the point where regret becomes irreparable.

Let's explore these ideas further:

Apology Over Eulogy:

- Apologizing when one has erred is a sign of responsibility and maturity. It's about stepping up to acknowledge a mistake and making amends before it's too late. While an apology can heal wounds and mend relationships, a eulogy symbolizes the end, often associated with lamenting what could have been done differently. The sentiment emphasizes timely resolution over delayed regret.

The Impersonal Aspect of Apology:

- "Don't take it personally" implies that when conflicts arise or mistakes are made, it's important to separate the personal feelings from the professional or situational context. This means not internalizing issues to the point of damaging self-esteem or letting emotions overpower judgment, but rather focusing on the issue at hand objectively.

Being Personable:

- Being personable, on the other hand, is about maintaining a positive and approachable demeanor. It's about being kind and empathetic in one's interactions. This human touch encourages a culture of openness and forgiveness, where team members feel comfortable admitting mistakes, knowing they will be received with understanding, rather than judgment.

Implications for Leadership and Relationships:

- For leaders, this philosophy underscores the importance of fostering a gracious and accountable culture. When leaders themselves practice apologizing, they set an example that it's acceptable not to be perfect, as long as one is willing to take responsibility and learn from their mistakes.
- In interpersonal relationships, this approach emphasizes treating others with respect and grace, especially when addressing difficulties. It promotes healing and growth over casting blame or harboring resentment.
- Additionally, in the context of not taking things personally, it advocates for resilience and emotional

intelligence, enabling individuals to negotiate misunderstandings and setbacks with composure and without damaging self-worth.

In essence, these ideas advocate for a compassionate, yet principled approach to interacting with others. It's about embracing our humanity—with all its flaws—while striving for personal and communal betterment. Through timely apologies, we can pave a path to resolution and unity, rather than traversing a road that leads to regret and lamentation. Combining these approaches reinforces a culture where people matter, and where personal accountability is seen not as a burden, but as an opportunity for growth and fostering genuine connections.

SL VII| *"When Respect Turns to Ridicule: its Disrespect" -GEM*

Introduction:

Respect is an essential element of social interaction and a cornerstone of healthy relationships, whether personal, professional, or social. It is a reflection of the value we assign to others and a measure of our character. Conversely, ridicule is an antithesis of respect – a corrosive force that undermines dignity and trust. The statement "When respect turns to ridicule, it's disrespect" encapsulates the fragile turning point where behavior shifts from validating to demeaning, highlighting the importance of maintaining respect even in disagreement.

Defining Respect and Ridicule:

Respect is the act of genuinely valuing and considering the feelings, wishes, rights, or traditions of others. It manifests in how we speak to and about others, the attention we pay to their opinions, and our willingness to treat others as equals. Ridicule, meanwhile, involves making someone the subject of scornful laughter, dismissing their perspective, or belittling their experiences – effectively stripping them of their dignity.

The Shift from Respect to Ridicule:

There are circumstances where the line between respect and ridicule can blur, such as in moments of anger, misunderstanding, or when hidden prejudices come to the fore. The descent from respect to ridicule often starts subtly – a sarcastic comment here, a dismissive gesture there – but can quickly escalate into outright disrespect.

The Effects of Ridicule:

The repercussions of ridicule are far-reaching. It can erode the foundation of trust and rapport that respect builds, leading to conflicts, alienation, and emotional distress. In the workplace, ridicule can sabotage teamwork and productivity, while in personal relationships, it can signal a breakdown in communication and breed resentment.

Navigating Disrespect:

Understanding how to navigate situations where respect may turn into ridicule is crucial for maintaining respectful interaction. It involves:

1. Self-awareness – Recognizing one's tendencies towards sarcasm or mockery and the triggers that evoke such behavior.

2. Emotional Regulation – Cultivating the ability to manage emotional responses to avoid lashing out with ridicule when challenged or upset.

3. Clear Communication – Expressing one's views without devaluing others, ensuring that criticisms are constructive rather than derisive.

4. Empathy – Making a conscious effort to understand the position of others and the potential impact of one's words or actions.

5. Apologizing – Owning up to moments when behavior crosses into ridicule and making amends to re-establish a basis of respect.

Conclusion:

The dichotomy between respect and ridicule serves as an important reminder of the care we must employ in our interactions with others. Ridicule, once initiated, can set a wheel of disconnection in motion, leading to consequences that resonate beyond the immediate context. Maintaining an environment of mutual respect requires vigilance, empathy, and the consistent application of principles that honor the inherent worth of every individual. After all, in a culture rich with respect, there is no room for ridicule to take root or thrive. Fostering respect over ridicule not only nurtures positive relationships but also upholds the fabric of a compassionate and understanding society.

SL VIII | "A Smile Goes Further than a Growl."
- GEM

The Power of Positive Expression

According to Forbes, an average happy adult smiles 40-50 times a day. A typical adult smiles only about 15-20 times a day.

Introduction:

In human interactions, non-verbal cues are as impactful, if not more so, than words themselves. Facial expressions are among the most expressive forms of non-verbal communication, conveying emotions and intentions. The maxim "A smile goes further than a growl" eloquently encapsulates the idea that positive expressions yield more favorable outcomes than negative ones. This maxim explores the transformative power of a smile in contrast to the repercussions of a growl and the broader implications each has on interpersonal relationships.

Every time you smile, you create a powerful chemical reaction. An article by Sarah Stevenson in

Psychology Today explains how it works: "When you smile, neuropeptides that help reduce stress are released. These neuropeptides send messages to your entire body when you're happy, excited, sad, or depressed. The feel-good neurotransmitters — dopamine, endorphins, and serotonin — are all released when a smile flashes across your face. This relaxes your body and can also lower your blood pressure and heart rate."

The Significance of Smiling:

Smiling is a universal gesture of goodwill, an innate expression that signifies joy, approachability, and benevolence. It is contagious; when we smile, we encourage others to smile back, thus fostering an atmosphere of friendliness and rapport. A smile can be disarming, breaking down barriers and communicating a readiness to interact positively. Psychological studies have shown that smiling not only lifts the mood of the person but also elevates the spirits of those around them, acting as a bridge to social connection.

Contrastingly, Growling as a Metaphor:

On the opposite end of the emotional spectrum, growling – while not often a literal human behavior – serves as a metaphor for expressions of anger, discontent, or aggressiveness. Such negative expressions can be off-putting and confrontational, creating distance rather than connection. A growl, whether through a frown, harsh words, or an aggressive stance, tends to elicit defensive or adverse reactions, escalating conflict rather than promoting understanding.

Interpersonal Dynamics:

In both personal and professional settings, a smile can facilitate cooperation and collaboration. It can ease tense moments, convey empathy, and even prevent misunderstandings. Smiling is particularly powerful in leadership, as it projects confidence while also expressing that leaders are approachable and considerate – crucial qualities for inspiring and motivating teams.

Conversely, growling can foster an environment of fear, resentment, and lowered morale. It may result in a lack of open communication and hinder the formation of meaningful connections. While there may be moments where showing displeasure is necessary, it must be balanced with positive reinforcement to avoid damaging relationships.

Social and Cultural Context:

It is also important to acknowledge the cultural nuances of smiling and expressions of sternness. What might be interpreted as a sign of friendliness in one culture could be misconstrued in another. Understanding these differences is key to effective and considerate communication across diverse groups.

Conclusion:

In the grand mosaic of human expression, a smile serves as a universal symbol of harmony and kinship that resonates deeper and reverberates longer than a growl ever could. While a growl may sometimes seem the easier, more instinctual response to challenges or dissatisfaction, it's a smile that opens doors, builds bridges, and sows the seeds of lasting positive impact. Whether it's to uplift ourselves, diffuse a difficult situation, or simply connect on a basic human level, a smile is a small gesture that moves us towards a brighter, more united existence. In summary, when we choose to smile rather than growl, we not only enhance our interactions but also contribute to a more amicable and understanding world.

SL XI| "The Economics of Kindness: Analyzing the Cost of Nastiness Versus the Savings of Niceness."

The maxim *"It costs you to be nasty; it saves you to be nice"- GEM* suggests that negative behavior has a tangible, often detrimental, impact on one's life, while a positive disposition can lead to benefits and savings. In this essay, we explore the concept that kindness can yield dividends in social capital, emotional well-being, and even financial outcomes, while nastiness can impose real costs.

The Price of Nastiness:

Engaging in unpleasant behavior can lead to a myriad of negative consequences. At a personal level, nastiness can result in stress and dissatisfaction, potentially escalating into mental and physical health issues. Socially, it can lead to strained relationships, loss of trust, and a tarnished reputation. From a career perspective, individuals who are known to be difficult or hostile may face professional setbacks like missed promotions or job termination. In financial terms, the repercussions of such setbacks could be significant.

Conversely, Professional Nastiness:

In certain professional contexts, there persists an argument that nastiness—or rather, ruthlessness—can be advantageous. Some people believe that being aggressive and forceful can lead to business success. However, this approach often overlooks the long-term costs, such as employee turnover, legal disputes, and lost opportunities due to burned bridges.

The Savings of Niceness:

On the flip side, being nice—or more aptly, being kind and respectful—can have numerous advantages. People who are pleasant to be around tend to form stronger relationships, both personally and professionally, leading to supportive networks. In the workplace, kind leaders often inspire loyalty and high performance, which can translate into better teamwork, productivity, and, ultimately, positive financial outcomes.

Furthermore, kindness has been linked to improved health and happiness. Acts of kindness release endorphins, which promote mood elevation and a sense of fulfillment. Happy individuals tend to be more productive, fostering a virtuous cycle of positive behavior and rewarding outcomes.

Economic Implications of Interpersonal Behavior:

The "economics" of our behavior factors greatly into our success and quality of life. People often underestimate the financial costs associated with negative behavior, such as the expenses related to health care, litigation, or recruitment. Conversely, the benefits of positive interaction, such as increased sales, customer loyalty, and collaborative innovation, positively impact the bottom line.

Intangibles and the Price of Values:

Beyond tangible outcomes, there's an intangible price to pay for nastiness or savings to gain from niceness—the value alignment with one's principles and the broader social good. Living in a way that aligns with core values like kindness, respect, and integrity often brings internal peace, which is hard to quantify but invaluable.

Conclusion:

While some may view the phrase "It costs you to be nasty; it saves you to be nice" as a simplistic assessment of human behavior, its implications are profound and far-reaching. The costs of nastiness manifest in various aspects of life, impacting health, relationships, and opportunities. Conversely, the benefits of niceness, often seen in the form of emotional well-being, social capital, and professional success, offer a persuasive argument for kindness as a way of life. As we navigate a world with increasing complexities, the economics of kindness serves as a reminder that our actions do affect our overall wealth—financially, socially, and spiritually.

"Don't you get mad at them; instead make them mad about you"-GEM.

SL X| The True Measure of Respect - Beyond Titles and Status

Introduction:

In a world often obsessed with rankings, positions, and titles, there exists a widespread notion that respect is a commodity tied to one's professional or social standing. However, the poignant assertion by GEM challenges this belief, underscoring a critical distinction between the superficiality of titles and the deeper, more intrinsic qualities that garner genuine admiration. ***"Title doesn't entitle you to respect"- GEM.*** It's not the status of a person that stands out; it's their stature," encapsulates a profound truth about the nature of respect and the qualities that truly make an individual worthy of it.

The Illusion of Titles:

Society frequently equates titles with success and, by extension, a certain entitlement to respect.

People in positions of power or with impressive job titles are often automatically accorded deference. However, this automatic association is misleading. A title is a label, a mere marker of a role or achievement, and does not reflect the character, ethics, or capabilities of the person holding it. While titles can be earned and can signify expertise or accomplishment in a particular field, they are not infallible indicators of a person's worthiness of respect.

Respect Earned Through Stature:

Stature, unlike status, is not granted through external validation or achieved through climbing a hierarchical ladder. It is cultivated internally and expressed through one's actions, behavior, and interactions with others. Stature is about the depth of character, the adherence to strong personal values, and the respect one shows to others regardless of their status. Individuals with true stature display qualities such as integrity, kindness, humility, and empathy. These are the people who earn respect naturally, as they contribute positively to the lives of others and uphold principles that resonate with the human spirit.

The Influence of Stature on Society:

Individuals who possess true stature have a lasting impact on society. They inspire others not by flaunting their titles, but by leading by example. They demonstrate that being a person of value is not contingent on recognition or authority but is about making meaningful contributions and fostering positive relationships. When society begins to value stature over status, we cultivate an environment where mutual respect and collaboration flourish over competition and self-aggrandizement.

Conclusion:

The words of GEM provide a thought-provoking perspective on the nature of respect and what truly matters when assessing the worth of an individual. As it becomes increasingly clear that titles and status are but superficial trappings, we are reminded that true respect is earned through one's stature—the unquantifiable essence of a person's character. It encourages a shift from a title-centric worldview to one that cherishes and rewards the intangible qualities that make us human. In the end, it is these qualities that leave a lasting legacy and truly stand out in the fabric of society.

MIND TIPS(EI)|PART III

Mind Tips is the Emotional Intelligence part of Leadership. Emotional intelligence (EI) refers to the capacity to comprehend and manage personal emotions as well as the emotions of others. It involves a keen understanding of one's internal emotional landscape and the ability to navigate through it, as well as interpreting and influencing the emotional states of others. The five cornerstone elements of EI include self-awareness, self-regulation, motivation, empathy, and social skills—all of which are essential for mastering one's emotions and remaining composed under pressure. This skill set not only offers personal benefits but is also regarded as a hallmark of effective leadership. The good news is that emotional intelligence is not an innate trait but a learnable skill that can be developed over time, enabling individuals to harness their emotional insights to lead and inspire those around them.

Mind Tips| The Dynamics of Focus: How Attention Drives Intentions

Introduction:

In the realm of leadership, the adage "where focus goes, energy flows" resonates with profound significance. This truth is encapsulated in the phrase "In Leadership, Attention Drives Intention," highlighting the critical role of focus in determining a leader's strategic pursuits and effective execution. This essay endeavors to dissect this phrase, examining how a leader's focus influences their intentions and, by extension, the trajectory of their organization.

The Theoretical Groundwork:

Attention in leadership can be likened to the lens of a camera, determining what is in the frame and what remains outside of it. The capacity of leaders to channel their attention effectively sets the stage for intention, which is the compass that points to their desired outcomes. Intention manifests as the concrete goals, objectives, and visions a leader sets for their team and organization. Without focused attention, the intention remains vague and directionless, whereas clear attention nurtures purposeful intention.

The Awareness-Action Loop:

Leadership entails a relentless cycle of awareness and action. A leader's attention guides their awareness, shaping their understanding of the organizational climate, market trends, internal dynamics, and external challenges. This awareness becomes the foundation upon which intentions are built decisions are made, goals are envisioned, and plans are laid down. Leaders who master the focus of their attention can create intentions that are informed, actionable, and aligned with their ultimate goals.

The Consequence of Scattered Attention:

A scattered focus leads to scattered intentions, and in the landscape of leadership, this spells a recipe for decline. When a leader's attention is fragmented, they risk spreading their resources too thinly, diluting their efforts, and fostering a culture of confusion. A leader must be judicious in what they choose to focus on, knowing that their concentrated attention can drive a team to achieve specific, meaningful objectives.

Cascade Effect of Leadership Attention:

The attention a leader invests in particular areas does not operate in isolation—it cascades throughout the organization. When a leader emphasizes customer satisfaction, for example, this intention permeates through to every level, driving initiatives to improve service. Similarly, a focus on innovation can invigorate a culture of creativity and experimentation. The intentions set by the leader based on focus areas become the guiding principles that shape the behavior and mindset of their subordinates.

The Criticality of Aligning Attention with Core Values:

Foundational to the concept of attention-driving intention is the leader's alignment with their core values. When a leader's focus is rooted in the values they advocate, the resulting intention is authentic and resonates more deeply with the team. This alignment empowers the leadership intention to not just direct actions but to inspire them, fostering a sense of shared purpose and collective pursuit.

Conclusion:

The essence of the phrase "In Leadership, Attention Drives Intention" spotlights a leadership competency that is at once subtle and powerful. A leader's focus determines where the collective energy of the organization is channeled. It is through deliberate and disciplined attention that a leader can carve out intentions that are both meaningful and impactful. Thus, effective leadership is an exercise in concentrated attention, revealing that true intention is not a matter of chance, but a choice that emerges from what leaders consciously choose to attend to.

Mind Tips II| "**Interesting is Interested**"-GEM

The maxim *"Interesting is interested"* within the context of the **GEM** model (***Goal, Execution, Monitoring***) touches on a powerful aspect of human interaction and engagement. Here's an exploration of how it ties into the model and what it signifies in both personal development and leadership:

Goal:

Setting interesting goals is important, but showing a clear, genuine interest in the goals themselves and the individuals involved in achieving them is crucial. When leaders are interested in the aspirations, passions, and motivations of their team members, they can tailor goals that not only align with organizational objectives but also resonate with the personal growth desires of their team.

Execution:

During the phase of execution, the interest leaders and team members show in the process of work – the challenges, the innovations, and solving problems – makes the journey towards the goal more engaging. This interest can breed creativity, collaboration, and commitment. Individuals who are interested in the work they do often find themselves being more interesting to others because their enthusiasm is infectious and encourages others to take an active part.

Monitoring:

The way leaders monitor progress is not just through tracking metrics and outcomes but also by showing interest in the ongoing development and experiences of their team. By being interested in their team's progress, struggles, and successes, leaders create an atmosphere of support and encouragement. This approach makes the monitoring phase less about judgment and more about learning and development, which is inherently more interesting for everyone involved.

Applying "Interesting is interested" to leadership beyond the GEM model:

Listening:

Leaders who listen with genuine interest to their team members – their ideas, feedback, and concerns – often find they garner far more interesting and diverse insights. This kind of empathetic listening fosters open communication and drives innovation.

Dialogue:

The conversations that leaders initiate and engage in reflect their interests. When those topics are interesting, it reflects a curiosity that can spark engaging, meaningful dialogues within the team.

Influence:

Leaders who show interest in learning and adapting will typically find their approach to be more interesting to others. People are drawn to leaders who are continually growing and who are interested in their environment, as they often bring new perspectives and insights.

In essence, the phrase suggests that to be perceived as interesting, one must be genuinely interested – in people, processes, and learning. It's the depth of interest that a leader shows that can galvanize a team, make goals more captivating, and transform the routine into the remarkable. When a leader is genuinely interested in the growth and well-being of their team, in the nuances of their work, and in the journey towards achieving their goals, the entire process becomes more interesting, encouraging increased engagement and dedication.

Mind Tips III| *"Listen for instruction, observe for obstructions, and speak for construction" -GEM.*

The maxim *"Listen for instruction, observe for obstructions, and speak for construction"* is a comprehensive approach that captures the essence of proactive communication and behavior within teams and organizations. This saying aligns perfectly with leadership principles and the dynamics of effective teamwork. Let's break down each part:

Listen for Instruction:

- This first part emphasizes the importance of active listening, which is pivotal in understanding directives, gaining knowledge, and receiving feedback. Leaders and team members who master the art of listening are better equipped to comprehend their tasks and the expectations set upon them. By listening, individuals gain clarity on their goals, their roles within the team, and the strategies needed for successful execution.

Observe for Obstructions:

- Observation is a critical skill for identifying potential hurdles that could impede progress. By being vigilant and aware of the environment, team members can preemptively spot challenges, concerns, or issues that may arise. Leaders who observe effectively can guide their teams through complexities, offering support or adapting plans as necessary. This careful attention to the operational landscape helps in the mitigation or elimination of obstacles.

Speak for Construction:

- The art of constructive communication is about framing responses, feedback, and dialogues in a way that builds up rather than tears down. When speaking, the focus should be on positive contributions that encourage growth, innovation, and collaboration. Leaders who speak for construction contribute to the development of a positive workplace culture, where team members feel valued and empowered to contribute their best.

Incorporating this tripartite approach ensures a balanced and proactive stance in professional and even personal environments:

For leaders, it underscores the importance of guiding with clarity (Emotional intelligence (EI) refers to the capacity to comprehend and manage personal emotions as well as the emotions of others. It involves a keen understanding of one's internal emotional landscape and the ability to navigate through it, as well as interpreting and influencing the emotional states of others. The five cornerstone elements of EI include self-awareness, self-regulation, motivation, empathy, and social skills—all of which are essential for mastering one's emotions and remaining composed under pressure. This skill set not only offers personal benefits but is also regarded as a hallmark of effective leadership. The good news is that emotional intelligence is not an innate trait but a learnable skill that can be developed over time, enabling individuals to harness their emotional insights to lead and inspire those around them.), strategy (observation), and positivity (construction). This approach fosters a culture of continuous learning, vigilance, and adaptive problem-solving.

For team members, it encourages a stance of readiness to learn, alertness to surroundings, and positivity in communication, all of which contribute to a functional, cohesive, and goal-oriented team dynamic.

"Listen for instruction, observe for obstructions, and speak for construction" is not just a catchy sentence; it is a philosophy of engagement that, when practiced, can significantly enhance the performance and morale of a team. It encapsulates a mindset of growth, awareness, and empowerment that drives both individual and collective success.

Mind Tips IV| "Beyond Emotions: The Pursuit of Purpose Amidst Inner Turbulence."

"Don't let how you're feeling keep you from fulfilling the assignment" GEM

Introduction:

Our emotions form the vibrant tapestry of our human experience, adding color and dimension to our daily lives. However, as powerful as they are, allowing emotions to govern our actions can be akin to navigating through a storm without a compass. Notably, when we are entrusted with an assignment – a task, a project, a mission, they more often act as the winds that steer us off course rather than the sails that propel us toward our destination. The essential lesson here is learning not to let how we're feeling prevent us from fulfilling our assignments.

The Power of Emotions:

Emotions are inherent elements of our psyche, capable of influencing our thoughts, behaviors, and decisions. They can serve as a source of invaluable insight, signaling our deepest values, fears, and desires. Feelings such as enthusiasm and passion

47

can drive us to exceed expectations, while fear and anxiety might caution us against potential risks. Nonetheless, despite their importance, emotions are temporary states, fluxes that ebb and flow like the tide, and should not singularly dictate our commitment to our assignments.

The Challenge of Emotional Mastery:

The ability to navigate our emotional landscape is quintessential to our success in any assignment. Mastery over our emotions doesn't imply suppression or denial; rather, it involves acknowledging feelings without letting them derail our progress. Emotional mastery requires a heightened sense of self-awareness, an understanding that while we cannot always control what we feel, we can control how we respond to those feelings.

Staying the Course:

When our emotions threaten to overwhelm our sense of duty, several strategies can anchor us. Firstly, we can engage in perspective-taking, reminding ourselves of the bigger picture and the importance of the assignment at hand. Setting clear, incremental goals can help maintain focus and provide a roadmap that guides us through emotional turbulence.

Another method is to establish habits and routines that support consistency. The discipline of routine can offer stability when emotions become tumultuous, enabling us to carry on with our responsibilities. Additionally, seeking supportive networks – mentors, colleagues, or friends who understand our vision – can offer encouragement and accountability, keeping us aligned with our assignments.

The Importance of Resilience:

Resilience is the capacity to bounce back from difficulties, and it plays a vital role when emotions threaten to impede our assignments. It's about being adaptable in the face of adversity and recovering quickly from emotional setbacks. Cultivating resilience can involve proactive stress management techniques, mindfulness practices, and a willingness to learn from each.

Mind Tips V| **"BAD ATTITUDES EMERGE IN THE ABSENCE OF GRATITUDE"-GEM**

This phrase suggests a philosophy of maintaining a positive and grateful outlook in the face of negativity or adversity. The idea is about countering negativity not with resentment or frustration but with a conscious choice to focus on the positives and express gratitude. This approach can diffuse tension, model constructive behavior, and potentially inspire a change in attitude for all parties involved. Would you like to delve into this topic further or explore a different subject?

When faced with a poor attitude from someone else, whether in a professional or personal context, it can be challenging to remain unaffected. However, choosing gratitude as a response is a powerful way to shift the dynamic and keep oneself anchored in a positive state of mind.

1. Gratitude as a Tool for Perspective

Gratitude can help you step back and appreciate the bigger picture, acknowledging that an individual's bad attitude is often not a reflection of your actions or values. It steers the focus away from negativity and toward elements of your life or situation that you're thankful for, reducing the emotional impact of someone else's behavior.

2. Influence Through Example

Demonstrating gratitude instead of mirroring a poor attitude can also catalyze change in others. Positivity can be infectious, and your display of appreciation can potentially encourage others to reconsider their approach and possibly adopt a more positive outlook.

3. Building Emotional Resilience

Gratitude isn't just about countering someone else's negativity; it bolsters your emotional resilience. By focusing on what's good in your life, you can often more easily cope with stress and recover from setbacks.

4. Maintaining Professionalism and Integrity

In work environments especially, exhibiting gratitude can be a testament to your professionalism. It allows you to maintain your integrity and stay above the fray of office politics or personal conflicts.

5. Fostering a Positive Environment

By choosing gratitude, you contribute to a positive environment. This can be incredibly impactful in group settings, where the emotions and attitudes of individuals can significantly influence the collective energy.

To cultivate a habit of gratitude, even more, you could keep a gratitude journal, practice mindfulness, or simply take a moment each day to reflect on what you're thankful for. Additionally, expressing gratitude to others, through words of appreciation or acts of kindness, not only lifts their spirits but reinforces your gratitude practice.

Would you like to focus on specific strategies to enhance gratitude, or explore its benefits and impacts in certain contexts, like the workplace or personal relationships?

Mind Tips VI| "Beyond Silence: Understanding the Dual Meanings of Quietude."

Introduction:
The maxim **_"Silence doesn't always mean consent, sometimes it's discontent"_** highlights the complexity of interpreting silence in communication. While silence is often taken as

acquiescence, it can also signify opposition, discomfort, or unease. This maxim delves into the nuances of silence, exploring how and why it may be used to express both agreement and dissent and discusses the importance of deciphering the unspoken messages it may convey.

The Ambiguity of Silence:

Silence is a multifaceted component of communication that can be as expressive as words. Its interpretation depends on context, cultural norms, body language, and the dynamics of the interaction. Understanding the layers behind silence is essential; assuming it indicates consent without seeking clarification can lead to misunderstandings and conflicts.

Silence as Consent:

In some cases, silence may imply agreement or a lack of objection. This can occur in situations where individuals feel adequately informed and in agreement with what is being proposed. Similarly, silence can be a tactic used to avoid confrontation or to give tacit approval without actively vocalizing support.

Silence as Discontent:

Conversely, silence can emanate from a place of discontent. This can take the form of withholding opinions out of fear of reprisal, a feeling of futility in expressing dissent, or a strategic pause to process information before responding. In such instances, silence acts as a protective mechanism or a subtle form of resistance.

The Consequences of Misinterpreting Silence:

Misinterpreting silence as consent, when it stems from discontent, can have significant consequences. In personal relationships, it may result in unresolved issues and resentment. In professional settings, it could lead to poor decision-making and reduced morale. Leaders, in particular, must be attuned to the potential meanings of silence to foster inclusive and open communication channels.

Navigating Silence:

Effective communication often involves 'reading the room' for nonverbal cues that accompany silence. Active listening, open-ended questions, and creating a safe environment for expression can encourage individuals to break the silence. Recognizing the power dynamics at play can also be critical, as those in lower positions may feel less comfortable speaking up.

Conclusion:

Silence is a complex phenomenon that cannot be boiled down to a single interpretation. It's essential to appreciate the duality of silence — as a form of consent or as an indication of discontent. Attentiveness to context and sensitivity to the possible reasons behind silence are key factors in accurately gauging its meaning. By embracing this nuanced understanding, we can strengthen our interactions and relationships, ensuring that silence, whether born from agreement or disagreement, is appropriately acknowledged, and addressed.

Mind Tips VII| Embracing Potential: How Acceptance of Ideas Cultivates Ideals

"Ideals are accepted when ideas aren't rejected" -GEM

The journey towards a utopian society is steered by the compass of human ideals, which are anchored deeply in the collective belief of what is possible. However, the birthplace of these ideals is the diverse marketplace of human ideas, where creative thought mingles with practical solutions. This principle explores how the acceptance of ideas is fundamental to the embracing and proliferation of ideals within societies, organizations, and personal growth.

Acceptance as the Seedbed of Transformation:

Ideas are transformative seeds, but they require a soil rich in acceptance to germinate and flourish. In environments where ideas are prematurely dismissed or ridiculed, the potential is stifled, and innovation is starved. Conversely, when ideas are nurtured with openness and considered without instant judgment, they can evolve into ideals that resonate with and inspire a wider audience.

The Dynamics of Rejection and Acceptance:

Rejection of ideas often stems from fear—fear of change, of the unknown, or failure. Consequently, this protective reflex can prevent societies and organizations from evolving. When ideas are not outright rejected but instead subjected to scrutiny and debate, they can be refined and strengthened, paving the way for broadly accepted and supported ideals.

The Process of Ideation:

Through the process of ideation, where brainstorming and diverse perspectives converge, ideas can be iterated upon. This process entails the acceptance of initial ideas as valid contributions, no matter how unorthodox they may seem. Only through such acceptance can the crystallization of more mature, sophisticated ideas emerge. This process echoes the scientific principle of hypothesizing: acceptance of an idea as a hypothesis allows for testing and iteration, leading to more refined theories.

Ideas as Catalysts for Ideals:

Often, great societal ideals are born from simple ideas that gain traction. For instance, the concept of equal rights for all started as a radical idea that faced much opposition. Over time, through persistent acceptance and championing of this idea by individuals and groups, it matured into a widely held ideal across much of the world.

The Power of Inclusivity:

In the realm of acceptance, inclusivity plays a significant role. It is not enough for singular authorities to accept ideas; greater power lies in collective acceptance. When various stakeholders are involved in the envisioning process, the resulting ideals have more depth and buy-in. Through the democratic vetting of ideas, where everyone's input is deemed valuable, ideals are more likely to be representative of and attainable by the collective.

The Role of Leadership:

Leaders have a profound impact on either endorsing or quashing the acceptance of ideas. Leaders guided by open-mindedness and who encourage free thought lay the groundwork for a culture where ideas can evolve into communal ideals. They recognize that the act of cultivating acceptance among their constituents can lead to a shared vision that motivates and unites.

Conclusion:

In conclusion, the adoption of ideals is less about the outright rejection or acceptance of any singular idea and more about the process through which ideas are allowed to develop, intermingle, and mature. A culture that values every contribution as a building block to a larger end is truly rich in potential. For ideals to be universally accepted, the precursor ideas must be given room to breathe, evolve, and intertwine with the tapestry of human experience. Only then can ideals be woven into the fabric of society in a meaningful and enduring way?

"Company Values are respected when staff is considered Valuable" - GEM

SP|SKILL PRO PART IV

Skill Pro | Professional skill consists of two types of skills, which are hard skills and soft skills. Soft skills – Soft skills on the other hand are usually self-taught and self-developed, and are becoming increasingly valuable to all employers, regardless of the type of industry they operate in. Hard skills, or technical skills, are learned through education or hands-on experience. These are concrete, measurable abilities that are often specific to a job. You can demonstrate your proficiency in hard skills through relevant certifications, portfolios, skill assessment tests, and completed work.

SP| Skill Pro. I

"The Power of Expectations: Fostering Success without Overt Correction"

The maxim **"Don't Correct, DO EXPECT"** alludes to an alternative approach to managing people, especially in leadership and personal development contexts. Rather than focusing on constant correction, this approach emphasizes the power of setting clear expectations. Here's a discussion of this concept:

Introduction

Traditional management and mentoring styles often hinge heavily on corrective feedback as a means to achieve desired outcomes. However, the maxim "Don't Correct, do EXPECT" suggests a transformative shift from this conventional approach. Instead, it advises that by setting clear, positive expectations, leaders and mentors can nurture a self-directed drive for excellence within their teams or protégés.

Rethinking Correction

Continuous correction can create an atmosphere of micromanagement, which can stifle creativity and initiative. When individuals are overly corrected, it can lead to a dependence on external guidance, leaving little room for self-assessment and personal growth. Moreover, frequent correction can undermine confidence and motivation, as individuals may feel perpetually inadequate or under scrutiny.

The Empowerment of Expectation

On the other hand, establishing robust expectations conveys a sense of trust and belief in an individual's abilities. When expectations are clear, people understand the standards they are meant to meet and can take ownership of their journey towards meeting them. Expectations act as a guiding north star, providing a clear direction without the need for constant realignment through correction.

Setting Effective Expectations

For expectations to be truly effective, they must be well-communicated, realistic, and attainable. They should challenge individuals to push their boundaries while still being within reach. Expectations must be aligned with the individual's or team's skills, resources, and the broader goals of the organization or endeavor.

It is also essential for leaders to be consistent in upholding these expectations and to provide the necessary support for individuals to meet them. This might include training, resources, mentorship, or simply a supportive environment that encourages experimentation and learning from mistakes.

The Role of Accountability

While the phrase suggests stepping away from correction, it does not imply a lack of accountability. Instead, the focus shifts to self-accountability, where individuals are encouraged to measure their performance against the set expectations. This encourages reflection and self-correction, which is often more powerful and enduring than externally imposed adjustments.

Leaders and mentors can facilitate this process by fostering a culture of open communication where feedback is sought and shared constructively, always to reinforce the agreed-upon expectations rather than criticize.

Celebrating Achievement

Emphasizing expectations creates opportunities to celebrate when they are met or exceeded. Recognition of success is a powerful motivator and reinforces the behaviors and outcomes aligned with the set standards. It also demonstrates the tangible results of meeting expectations, which can further drive commitment and high performance.

Conclusion: Embracing a Culture of Expectation

The maxim "Don't Correct, do EXPECT" is a gem of wisdom that encapsulates the effectiveness of a leadership and development strategy rooted in empowerment rather than enforcement. By setting and maintaining clear expectations, leaders can cultivate a culture where individuals are motivated by a shared vision of success and are actively engaged in their growth journey.

This approach fosters a sense of agency, competence, and achievement that goes beyond the superficial compliance that correction often yields. Ultimately, a focus on expectation lays the groundwork for a collaborative and aspirational environment, where greatness is not just corrected into being, but expected—and hence, realized with greater fulfillment and agency.

SP| Skill Pro II

"Bridging the Gap between Expectation and Reality: The Deming Approach"

The maxim "You Inspect what you expect," often associated with the influential management thinker W. Edwards Deming, embodies a core principle of quality and performance management. It emphasizes the importance of not only setting expectations but also actively measuring and checking to ensure those expectations are met. Here's an exploration of this concept:

Introduction

In the pursuit of excellence, both in business and personal growth, clear expectations are fundamental. However, as W. Edwards Deming insightfully observed, "You Inspect what you expect," pointing out that without a mechanism to monitor outcomes, expectations remain mere aspirations. This motto calls for a hands-on approach to ensure that the set standards are being achieved.

The Cycle of Continuous Improvement

Deming is known for his work in quality management and continuous improvement. Among his many contributions is the Deming Cycle, or PDCA (Plan-Do-Check-Act), which is a systematic series of steps for ongoing improvement. The "Check" phase of this cycle is particularly relevant to the maxim; it's the point at which the system or outcome is inspected to ascertain alignment with expectations.

Setting the Standard

Expectations function as benchmarks for performance and outputs, but they alone do not guarantee that the objectives will be achieved. Careful and systematic inspection of the processes and outcomes ensures that expectations serve as operational standards rather than as mere hopes.

Inspection as Accountability

Regular inspection against expectations creates a culture of accountability. It sends a clear message that the organization is serious about its standards, and it reinforces the commitment to those standards by demonstrating a willingness to invest time and resources into the evaluation process.

Data-Driven Management

Deming was a proponent of using statistical methods to analyze processes and improve quality. "You Inspect what you expect" underscores the importance of gathering data and evidence when evaluating performance. In an era where data-driven decisions are pivotal, measuring performance against expectations becomes imperative for success.

Recognizing and Resolving Discrepancies

When inspection reveals a gap between what is expected and what is being delivered, it provides an opportunity to take corrective action—one cannot fix what one does not measure. This aspect of inspection is key to maintaining high standards and fostering a culture of continual improvement. When performance falls short of expectations, root cause analysis and corrective measures can be implemented to bridge the gap.

Encouraging Improvement through Feedback

The process of inspection also functions as a feedback loop to the people or teams involved. Positive feedback can reinforce good practices, while constructive feedback can guide improvements. This continuous loop ensures that expectations are communicated, understood, and acted upon, driving progress and mastery.

Conclusion: The Critical Role of Inspection in Excellence

"You Inspect what you expect" transcends industries and applications to stand as a timeless principle of effective management and performance. It reminds us that for any goal, system, or process, having clear expectations is only the starting point. To truly achieve and maintain high standards, one must actively inspect and engage with the outcomes, making adjustments as necessary to align reality with aspiration.

In embracing this principle, organizations can ensure that their objectives are met with precision and efficiency, while individuals can apply it as a principle for accountability and self-improvement on the path to personal excellence.

SP| Skill Pro III

"Follow Up for Follow Through: The GEM of Realizing Goals"

The maxim *"Follow Up for Follow Through"* can be turned into a comprehensive model for success known as the **GEM (*Goal, Execution, Monitoring*)** framework. This approach provides a detailed strategy to ensure that one's intentions are not only set in motion but are also brought to fruition through dedication, systematic action, and continuous oversight. Let's delve deeper into the intricacies of the GEM model:

Introduction

In the personal and professional quest for success, it's not enough to have a vision; one must cultivate the tenacity and strategic oversight to see that vision materialize. "Follow Up for Follow Through" articulates the essence of this process, encapsulating the commitment required to transition goals from the ideation phase to the realm of accomplishment. The GEM (Goal, Execution, Monitoring) model provides a structured approach to achieving this transformation.

Goal: The Bedrock of Ambition

The clarity and definition of a goal are what gives it power. A well-articulated goal acts as the foundation for all subsequent actions and decisions. It should encapsulate the desired outcome and resonate with the core values and ambitions of the individual or organization setting it.

Setting SMART Goals

To make follow-up effective, goals should be SMART: Specific, Measurable, Achievable, Relevant, and Time-bound. This framework ensures that a goal is not only clear and quantifiable but also realistic and bound to a timeline that promotes urgency and focus.

Visioning and Commitment

Goal-setting also involves visualizing the end state and committing to the pursuit. The more vividly one can picture the outcome, the stronger the intrinsic motivation to achieve that goal, providing a psychological boost to the rigors of follow-through.

Execution: The Journey from Plan to Practice

Meticulously crafting an action plan is where many falter in the journey toward goal realization. Execution is where theoretical potential meets practical application—it's about taking concrete steps towards your objectives.

Milestones and Action Items

Effective execution requires breaking down the path to your goal into tangible milestones and individual action items. This not only simplifies the process but also allows for more manageable and trackable progressions.

Resource Allocation and Delegation

Identifying the necessary resources, including time, money, and human capital, is crucial. Equally important is assigning responsibility for tasks to the right people or ensuring that one can manage these tasks personally.

Agility and Resilience in Execution

One of the keys to successful execution is the ability to stay agile and resilient. Projects and goals are dynamic—obstacles arise, and conditions change. Execution plans must, therefore, be adaptable to such changes without the core goal being compromised.

Monitoring: The Critical Role of Vigilance

Monitoring is what binds the goal and its execution together. It is an ongoing commitment to ensure fidelity to the original objective and to gauge the effectiveness of the implementation.

Continuous Evaluation and Reporting

Regular monitoring involves tracking progress against the established milestones, evaluating the results, and generating reports that provide insight into the health and trajectory of the project or goal.

Feedback and Corrective Actions

Monitoring should not be a passive activity; it should actively inform the goal-pursuit process. When discrepancies arise between expectations and reality, feedback loops must be enacted to address these issues and to implement corrective actions swiftly.

Celebrating Successes and Learning from Failures

An often-overlooked aspect of monitoring is acknowledging both the successes and failures along the way. Celebrating small wins promotes morale and motivation while dissecting failures provides powerful learning opportunities.

Conclusion: The Synergy of GEM

By embracing the "Follow Up for Follow Through" methodology, distilled into the GEM model, one steps into a mindset and practice that synergizes goal setting, execution, and monitoring into a powerful engine for achievement. It's a testament to the fact that the realization of goals is an active and dynamic process, marked by ongoing engagement, strategic action, and vigilance.

Whether applied to individual growth, project management, team leadership, or broad organizational strategy, the extended application of "Follow Up for Follow Through" via the GEM framework shines as a beacon of guiding principles for realizing ambitions and propelling success. Through this meticulous and intentional approach, the path from aspiration to actualization is charted with precision and purpose—affirming that diligent follow-up is vital for successful follow-through.

SP | Skill Pro IV

"Specificity leads to simplicity."

encapsulates the idea that when objectives, plans, or tasks are specific and clearly defined, they become easier to understand and execute. This principle is very much in alignment with the GEM model – Goal, Execution, Monitoring – as it suggests that specificity in each of these areas can simplify the process of achieving success.

Let's break down how specificity leads to simplicity within the context of the GEM model:

Goal:

Specific Goals:

Clear, specific goals eliminate ambiguity and confusion about what is to be achieved. When a goal is well-defined, it becomes easier to communicate to all stakeholders and simplifies the process of rallying a team around that goal.

Simple Direction:

The simplicity derived from a specific goal is that it provides a single direction in which all efforts should be channeled. This clarity allows team members to concentrate their efforts without being sidetracked by unrelated tasks or projects.

Execution:

Specific Plans:

Execution begins with a plan that outlines specific actions to be taken to achieve the goal. When these actions are detailed and precise, it reduces the chances of misinterpretation and error in carrying out the steps required to move forward.

Simple Process:

Specificity in execution streamlines the process. With clear directives, individuals can work more independently and confidently, knowing exactly what is expected of them. This can also simplify decision-making, as each choice can be weighed against clearly outlined criteria that lead toward the goal.

Monitoring:

Specific Metrics:

To monitor progress effectively, specific metrics need to be established. These metrics should be directly tied to the goal and should provide clear indicators of progress or areas in need of attention.

Simple Evaluation:

With specific metrics, evaluating progress is simplified. It becomes easier to make informed decisions about whether to continue on the current path, to adjust tactics, or to realize when the goal has been met. It also simplifies reporting to stakeholders, as the criteria for success are well-known and agreed upon.

In summary, specificity leads to simplicity by removing excess and focusing on what is essential. It cuts through confusion, reduces complexity, and provides a roadmap that is easy to follow. In the context of the GEM model, specificity is the tool that sharpens focus on the Goal, refines the Execution plan, and clarifies the Monitoring process, thereby simplifying the path to success.

SP | Skill Pro V

"First you must hear and then you will be heard" -GEM

underlines the importance of empathetic listening in communication, especially in leadership and personal relationships. Empathetic listening is about truly understanding the speaker's message, both intellectually and emotionally, before responding or seeking to be understood. This involves fully concentrating on the speaker, acknowledging their feelings, and showing genuine interest in their perspectives and experiences.

This practice goes beyond simply waiting for one's turn to speak or preparing a reply while someone else is talking. Instead, it involves an active process where the listener validates the speaker's emotions and experiences, creating a space where they feel understood and respected.

Here's why empathetic listening is so valuable:

Intellectual and Emotional Focus:

Intellectual focus involves understanding the content of the message and the logic behind the speaker's thoughts or arguments. Emotional focus requires the listener to tune into the speaker's feelings, which might be explicitly expressed or subtly conveyed through tone, body language, and facial expressions.

- By engaging both intellectually and emotionally, the listener gains a deeper comprehension of the speaker's point of view and can provide a more thoughtful and relevant response.

Responding with Empathy:

In contrast to trading anecdotes, empathetic listening prioritizes the speaker's narrative. Rather than diverting the focus to one's own similar experiences, the listener stays present with the speaker's story, showing that they value the speaker's unique perspective.

Responses in empathetic listening often involve reflective statements that encapsulate the speaker's expressed thoughts and feelings, which helps the speaker feel truly heard and understood.

Validation of Experience:

- Validating the speaker's experience does not mean agreeing with them on every point; rather, it acknowledges their right to their feelings and perspectives. This validation is crucial for building trust and can foster open, honest communication.
- Recognizing and validating another's experiences does not detract from one's own experiences or expectations. It merely creates a supportive environment for dialogue and can lead to mutual understanding even when differences exist.

Benefits in Leadership and Relationships:

In leadership, empathetic listening is a powerful tool for inspiring and motivating teams. It builds rapport and trust, which are foundational for effective teamwork and collaboration.

In personal relationships, this type of listening strengthens connections, as it shows care and respect for the other person's inner world, reinforcing the bond between individuals.

Implications for Productivity and Harmony:

When people feel heard, they are more likely to be cooperative and open-minded, which can lead to more productive and harmonious interactions. This builds a culture of respect where individuals are more inclined to listen to and consider alternate viewpoints.

In conflict resolution, empathetic listening can diffuse tension and help reach a shared understanding or compromise, as parties are more willing to reciprocate empathy when they are listened to empathetically.

The ability to listen empathetically is essential for effective communication and leadership. It involves a delicate balance between understanding the intellectual content and connecting with the emotional context of what is being said. True empathetic listening fosters an inclusive atmosphere where all parties can feel safe to express themselves and collaborative solutions can be reached that respect the needs and expectations of everyone involved.

SP | Skill Pro Vl

Embracing the Dual Nature of Leadership: Beyond Authority to Active Engagement

"Leadership is not just about being in charge, it's about being able to take charge also."-GEM.

In a world swarming with titles and positions, the true essence of leadership often becomes blurred and misconceived. The maxim above cuts through the noise to remind us that leadership isn't just about wielding power from a lofty position; it's about stepping up to embrace responsibilities, about being as willing to listen and adapt as to direct and enforce.

The Misinterpreted Mantle of Leadership

Historically, being 'in charge' has been synonymous with issuing orders, controlling resources, and maintaining a stately distance from the 'doers'. This image paints leaders as gatekeepers of power, not as participants in the struggle toward a collective aspiration. It's an allure that can trap those new to leadership, fooling them into believing that authority alone makes a leader.

The Crucial Shift: From Power to Participation:

The reality is far more action-oriented. To lead is not just to sit at the head of the table, but to be the pulse that energizes dialogues, the hand that offers support, and the beacon that guides through the darkness. True leaders are those who can 'take charge,' who don't shy away from the front lines, and who stand shoulder to shoulder with their team when challenges arise.

The Balance of Command and Collaboration:

Leadership involves a delicate balance. It requires the foresight to delegate effectively and the wisdom to know when personal intervention is necessary. It's about navigating the dual roles of visionary and executor, of thought leader and action-taker. A leader must blend the confidence to make tough calls with the vulnerability to admit missteps.

Engaging with Empathy and Accountability:

Taking charge involves being both a beacon of hope and a pillar of reliability. It incorporates an empathetic approach that values the team's input and recognizes their contributions. It also encapsulates the willingness to be accountable, to own up to the outcomes, whether they're triumphs or setbacks, and to learn from each experience.

Cultivating a Culture of Shared Leadership:

Perhaps the most transformative aspect of this dual leadership approach is its ability to inspire others. When a leader is seen sharing the load, it creates a powerful model for others to emulate. It cultivates an environment where each member feels empowered to step up, take initiative, and demonstrate leadership.

Conclusion

The quote at the beginning of this piece doesn't just define leadership - it challenges it. It pushes past the comfortable recesses of commanding from behind closed doors to a place where leaders are active, engaged, and as accountable as any team member. In this dynamic dance of guiding and participating, dictating and listening, enforcing and being on the ground, leadership is redefined not as a title held but as a role lived – deeply, authentically, and courageously.

SP | Skill Pro VII

"Trust No One, Entrust Everyone" - GEM
Balancing Caution with Empowerment

Introduction:

The paradoxical maxim, "Trust no one, entrust everyone," captures a complex philosophy of interpersonal dynamics, especially prevalent in leadership and management. It suggests a cautious approach to trust—being wary of placing complete confidence in others blindly—while advocating for the distribution of responsibility and the empowerment of individuals. This essay delves into the nuanced balance between skepticism and the delegation of trust, examining the implications for personal growth, team dynamics, and organizational success.

Understanding Trust and Entrusting:

Trust involves a belief in the reliability, truth, ability, or strength of someone. It is a delicate, intangible commodity that takes time to build but can be shattered in an instant. To entrust, however, is to assign responsibility or charge of something to someone, which is a core principle of effective leadership and team management, regardless of the level of interpersonal trust involved.

Dangers of Blind Trust:

Blindly trusting anyone without due diligence or evidence of their trustworthiness can be naive and potentially harmful. Excessive trust can lead to exploitation, disappointment, or betrayal, as it may not always be met with the same level of integrity by others.

Benefits of Entrusting:

Conversely, entrusting others with tasks or responsibilities is crucial for fostering a sense of ownership, accountability, and personal development. It can lead to increased engagement, permit diverse ideas to flourish, and encourage individuals to rise to the occasion. By sharing responsibility, leaders can also facilitate a learning environment where successes are celebrated, and failures are treated as learning opportunities.

Balance in Leadership:

The dichotomy of 'trust no one, entrust everyone' suggests leaders should be discerning, verifying trustworthiness through consistent actions over time, while remaining open to the potential of their team members. It requires a balance of insight to protect against the pitfalls of misplaced trust and the wisdom to cultivate talent through empowerment.

In practice, this philosophy encourages setting clear expectations, establishing transparent processes, and implementing checks and balances. It encompasses the idea that while individuals should be empowered with responsibilities, a framework should be in place to monitor performance and ensure accountability without stifling independence and growth.

Final Thoughts:

In essence, this statement prompts us to be strategic in how we place our trust, exercise vigilance without being unreasonably distrustful, and empower others with the freedom to act, learn, and prove their capabilities. The art of leading effectively lies in navigating this balance—ensuring that while trust is earned and re-evaluated continuously, everyone is given a chance to demonstrate their potential through the tasks they are entrusted with. Through this delicate interplay, we can create resilient, dynamic, and trustworthy teams, where members are not only entrusted but become truly trustworthy.

Skill Pro VIII

"Reliability and Credibility: Companions to Responsibility, Not Replacements"

Introduction:

The maxim ***"Reliability and credibility don't excuse responsibility" GEM*** refers to the idea that while being reliable and credible are valuable traits, they should not be seen as a substitute for taking responsibility. It emphasizes the comprehensive nature of accountability in personal and professional contexts. This maxim examines the interplay between these traits and the holistic commitment required for genuine responsibility.

Reliability, Credibility, and Their Limits:

Reliability refers to the consistency of a person's actions and the ability to deliver on promises. Credibility is built on a foundation of trust and is reflective of a person's perceived integrity and reputation. However, the existence of these qualities in a person or organization does not mitigate the need to assume full responsibility for actions and decisions.

The Fallacy of Complacency:

Individuals or organizations often rest on the laurels of past achievements of reliability and credibility. This complacency can lead to a false sense of security, where responsibility may become diluted or neglected. A reputation for past success does not inherently resolve current issues or absolve from the responsibility of future endeavors.

The Essence of True Responsibility:

True responsibility entails a proactive and ongoing commitment to the duties one has within any role or relationship. It means being answerable for the outcomes of one's actions, regardless of one's track record. It involves facing the consequences, both good and bad, and taking corrective action when necessary while learning and growing from each situation.

Integrating Reliability, Credibility, and Responsibility:

The integration of reliability and credibility with responsibility can result in a harmonious alignment where each quality reinforces the others. Reliability can lead to predictability in taking responsibility, and credibility can strengthen the trust stakeholders have that responsibilities will be met. However, neither can take the place of direct accountable action.

Case Examples:

Examples in business can include a company that has reliably produced quality products but is suddenly faced with a product recall. The company's credibility may buffer initial reactions, but it will be its responsible handling of the recall—addressing safety concerns and compensating customers—that ultimately defines its reputation. Similarly, in personal relationships, a person known to be reliable must still take responsibility for their mistakes, as trust in relationships is continually recalibrated based on current actions, not just past behavior.

Conclusion:

The fusion of reliability and credibility contributes significantly to the perception of responsibility but does not excuse individuals or organizations from their duty to remain accountable. It is through the consistent and active embrace of responsibility that the true measure of an individual's or an entity's character is revealed. Reliability and credibility are qualities that can certainly enhance responsibility, but they can never replace the act of being responsible. By understanding and acting on this distinction, individuals and organizations alike can foster a culture of accountability and trustworthiness that stands the test of time.

SP | Skill Pro IX

The Whole Sum of Parts: Why Half Measures Yield No Value

"Half of Nothing is Still Nothing" - Anonymous

Introduction:

The prolific statement "Half of nothing is still nothing" holds a profound truth that transcends mathematical logic and enters the realm of philosophy, work ethic, and personal growth. It speaks to the concept of commitment and the futility of half-hearted efforts. This essay explores the significance of fully engaging in endeavors and the implication of partial efforts in various aspects of life.

The Illusion of Partial Investment:

Half measures can be seen in situations where individuals or organizations invest resources, time, or effort into an endeavor but fail to do so completely. This can be due to a variety of reasons, such as fear of failure, lack of resources, or a fundamental misunderstanding of what is required. The illusion that partial investment can lead to some measure of success often results in wasted potential and unachieved goals.

The Mathematics of Effort:

Mathematically, half of zero is indeed zero, and this principle applies metaphorically as well. A task half done often bears no fruit— particularly in tasks where a complete process is necessary to produce any outcome. In many real-world cases, a commitment that does not see an endeavor through to its entirety is tantamount to not having begun at all. For instance, constructing half a bridge does not facilitate crossing a river, and half a degree does not grant the title or qualification that comes with full academic certification.

Holistic Commitment and Success:

Success in most areas requires a holistic commitment. For instance, in relationships, it is a full investment of trust, time, and effort that yields a strong bond. In businesses, it is the complete and thorough execution of ideas and strategies that leads to growth and profitability. In personal development, it is the unwavering commitment to self-improvement and goal realization that brings about meaningful change.

The Ripple Effects of Half Measures:

Half-hearted efforts can have ripple effects beyond the immediate outcome. They can damage credibility, erode trust, and undermine the integrity of processes and systems. They indicate a lack of dedication, which can be demoralizing to teams and individuals alike, further impeding progress and collaboration.

Elevating from Nothing to Something:

Moving from 'nothing' to 'something' demands a full-hearted approach. This involves setting clear objectives, engaging wholeheartedly with challenges, and persevering through difficulties. It means expecting and preparing for full engagement, not settling for partial victories or incomplete solutions.

Conclusion:

The adage "Half of nothing is still nothing" serves as a pertinent reminder that anything worth doing is worth doing fully. Partial efforts lead nowhere and are ultimately equivalent to inaction. By recognizing the importance of complete engagement and eschewing half measures, we can transform nothing into something substantial and meaningful, achieving success that is not just quantifiable but felt in its entirety. Whether in professional endeavors, personal goals, or interpersonal relationships, it is the wholehearted commitment that bridges the gap from the absence of achievement to the fulfillment of potential. In essence, until we submit we will not commit!

Skill Pro X

"The Mastery of Delegation: Key to Administrative Efficacy"

Introduction:

Effective administration is a cornerstone of successful organizations. Central to this role is the ability to delegate efficiently, which is the art of entrusting tasks and authority to others. The maxim ***"An effective administrator is an efficient delegator" -GEM*** This maxim encapsulates the idea that a key quality of good leaders is their ability to appropriately assign responsibilities to their team members, not only to manage the workload but also to empower and develop employees.

The Essence of Efficient Delegation:

Efficient delegation involves more than simply handing off tasks; it's about identifying the right tasks to delegate, choosing capable individuals, communicating expectations clearly, and providing the necessary support and resources. It's a strategic function that necessitates understanding the strengths and development needs of team members and aligning these with organizational objectives.

Benefits of Delegation:

1. Time Management: Delegation frees up administrators' time to focus on high-level planning and decision-making.
2. Employee Development: Assigning responsibilities to subordinates contributes to their professional growth and job satisfaction.
3. Increased Productivity: With tasks distributed appropriately, work gets done more efficiently, leading to higher productivity.
4. Improved Team Dynamics: Delegation can foster a sense of trust and collaboration within a team.

The Art of Choosing What to Delegate:

An effective administrator must know what tasks to delegate. Activities that are suitable for delegation typically include routine operations, technical tasks, and projects where other team members have the expertise. However, responsibility for critical decision-making, crisis management, and sensitive issues often remains with the administrator.

Matching Tasks with Talents:

The key to efficient delegation is matching the tasks at hand with the talents of the staff. This requires an intimate knowledge of each team member's skills, aspirations, and capacity for additional responsibilities. It also implies fair and impartial assessment when assigning tasks, considering the team's dynamics and the individual's professional development plan.

Providing Adequate Resources and Support:

An administrator must ensure that employees are adequately equipped to take on delegated responsibilities. This means providing the necessary resources, training, and support. It also entails setting up clear lines of communication and establishing a framework for accountability.

The Challenges of Delegation:

Despite its benefits, delegation can pose challenges. The fear of loss of control, concern about the capabilities of subordinates, and difficulty in letting go of tasks can prevent administrators from delegating effectively. Overcoming these challenges requires trust in the team and a willingness to accept that mistakes may happen as part of the learning process.

Conclusion:

Indeed, an effective administrator is an efficient delegator. Through strategic delegation, administrators can enhance team capabilities, streamline operations, and foster a collaborative work environment. By mastering the nuances of delegation—knowing what, when, and to whom to delegate—administrators empower themselves and their teams, thereby driving organizational success. The savvy administrator recognizes that delegation is not just a managerial task but an essential leadership skill that when executed with care and precision, results in a more dynamic, capable, and engaged workforce.

"Pass it on so you don't pass out" -GEM

Skill Pro XI

"Systems only work when you work within the systems"-GEM

Systems are the bedrock of efficiency and productivity in various aspects of life, from the machinery of government to the operations of a business and even the routines of personal habits. The maxim "Systems only work when you work within the systems" underscores the fundamental principle that the effectiveness of any system hinges on the active and knowledgeable participation of the individuals it is designed to serve or govern.

The Essence of Systems

A system is an organized set of principles or procedures according to which something is done; an intricate network of components working in harmony to achieve a specific goal. Systems are everywhere — in nature, technology, society, and at the core of our daily interactions and operations.

Systems in Action

Consider the traffic system, a complex arrangement of rules, signals, and conduct that, when adhered to, allows for the orderly flow of vehicles and pedestrians. Similarly, an organization might have a system for processing paperwork, which requires steps to be followed in sequence for successful completion. When people fail to work within these established systems, the result is often confusion, delays, and even disaster.

The Role of Individual Participation

Systems are, by design, larger than the individuals within them. However, the success of any system critically depends on individual adherence and cooperation. Simply put, no matter how perfectly a system is designed, it becomes virtually ineffective if the people it is intended to organize or benefit do not engage with it properly.

Challenges and Solutions

One of the challenges faced is that systems can be rigid, complicated, or poorly communicated, making it difficult for people to work within them effectively. To counteract this, system designers must strive for clarity, simplicity, and accessibility. Onboarding, training, and continuous education play critical roles in ensuring individuals understand how to function within the system.

Recognition of Exceptions

It's important to acknowledge that systems, while crucial, are not infallible. There may be instances when working outside the established system is necessary — due to unforeseen circumstances or because the system is flawed. In these situations, identifying the shortcomings and adapting the system to better meet the needs of its users is vital.

The Human Element

At the heart of any system is the human element. Creating a culture where members are incentivized to work within the given framework can increase adherence and effectiveness. Recognizing and rewarding those who contribute positively to the system not only bolsters engagement but also motivates others to follow suit.

Conclusion

In conclusion, the maxim "Systems only work when you work within the systems" serves as a reminder of the interplay between individual participation and systemic effectiveness. For systems to fulfill their intended purpose, they require the consistent and informed actions of the people who operate within them. It is a call to action for both system creators and users alike to continuously engage, refine, and respect the structures that help organize our complex world. Remember shortcuts cut short your bonus and or your tenure!

Skill Pro XII

"Hard to Manipulate A Template"- GEM

In an age where information is abundant and simultaneously complex, the need for structures that guide behavior and decisions is increasingly important. The maxim "Hard to manipulate when there's a template" by GEM encapsulates a profound understanding of how predefined frameworks can provide stability and guard against undue influence. This chapter will explore the implications of this maxim and how templates serve as a bulwark against manipulation in various contexts.

Understanding Templates

A template is a pattern or model that is used as a guide for creating something. In a broader sense, it serves as a fixed reference point that standardizes processes, behaviors, or operations. Templates can be found in diverse fields, from document creation to decision-making protocols and behavioral guidelines.

The Shield Against Manipulation

To manipulate is to influence or control someone or something to one's advantage, oftentimes unfairly or dishonestly. In the face of manipulation tactics, a template acts as a shield, providing a clear outline or set of guidelines that subvert attempts at improper influence. Templates instill consistency and uniformity that make it challenging for manipulation to take root because there is less room for alternative interpretations or deviations.

Templates in Practice

In the context of a contractual agreement, for example, a well-crafted template can protect parties from the pitfalls of vague or manipulative clauses. The structure it provides ensures that the terms are transparent and leaves little wiggle room for exploitation. Similarly, in a scientific environment, research templates uphold the integrity of studies by ensuring that experiments follow a consistent methodology, which guards against the manipulation of data or results.

Flexibility Within Framework

While templates are protective measures against manipulation, they must also possess a level of flexibility to remain relevant and useful. A rigid template that doesn't allow for contextual adjustments can become obsolete or excessively restrictive. Therefore, while it's essential to have a solid framework in place, there must be provisions for growth and evolution within these templates to accommodate the nuances of real-world applications.

Ethical and Moral Dimensions

Adhering to a template also has ethical and moral dimensions. It fosters a culture of integrity and transparency. As individuals and organizations commit to standardized procedures and guidelines, the likelihood of manipulative practices diminishes, cultivating an environment where fairness and honesty prevail.

The Human Element

However, reliance on templates should not dismiss the importance of critical thinking and discernment. Human judgment is vital when a situation falls outside of a template's scope or when the template itself needs to be evaluated for its efficacy and fairness. Thus, while templates serve as a protective measure, they should operate alongside, not instead, human insight.

Conclusion

The maxim "Hard to manipulate when there's a template" highlights the importance of having a well-defined structure as an antidote to manipulation. Templates serve as a guiding hand that not only maintains order but also enforces ethical conduct. In a world where uncertainty can bring about the opportunity for manipulation, a strong, adaptable template can ensure that integrity is upheld. This chapter underscores the interplay between steadfast guidelines and the adaptive, discerning human spirit that together provide a foundation resistant to manipulation. There's no need to contemplate with an effective template!

Skill Pro XIII

"A company's greatest resource is resourcefulness."
- GEM

In today's fast-paced and ever-evolving business landscape, the maxim "A company's greatest resource is resourcefulness" sheds light on an indispensable trait that distinguishes successful organizations from the rest. This essay delves into the multifaceted concept of resourcefulness and its pivotal role as the most valuable asset a company can possess.

The Concept of Resourcefulness

Resourcefulness is the ability to find quick and clever ways to overcome difficulties. It involves creativity, adaptability, and the capacity to leverage available resources effectively. Being resourceful means harnessing problem-solving skills to navigate challenges, innovating with limited resources, and turning potential setbacks into opportunities.

The Limitations of Tangible Assets

Traditionally, it has been perceived that a company's resources such as capital, raw materials, and technology are the cornerstones of its growth and success. While these resources are certainly important, they are also finite and can be acquired by competitors. Moreover, material resources themselves do not guarantee success; they must be managed and utilized smartly, which is where resourcefulness comes into play.

Resourcefulness as a Dynamic Driver

A resourceful company is characterized by its dynamic culture that encourages initiative and innovation. Resourceful companies are adept at making the most of what they have, often achieving more with less. They are resilient in the face of difficulties and agile enough to pivot when necessary. This agility allows them to stay ahead in a competitive market by continuously finding new and effective ways to meet the demands of their customers and clients.

Human Capital and Resourcefulness

At the heart of a resourceful company are its people—employees who possess the skills, knowledge, and creativity to maximize the potential of their organization. The value of human capital cannot be understated, as it is the employees' resourcefulness that catalyzes the growth and evolution of a company. Therefore, fostering a work environment that nurtures creative thinking, learning, and problem-solving is essential for cultivating the resourcefulness of a workforce.

The Edge in Innovation

Resourcefulness is also synonymous with innovation. Companies renowned for being innovative, such as Apple or Tesla, attribute much of their success to their ability to think outside the box and approach problems with a resourceful mindset. This approach not only helps in designing groundbreaking products and services but also streamlines internal processes, cutting costs and improving efficiency.

Learning from Setbacks

A key aspect of resourcefulness is the ability to learn from setbacks rather than be defeated by them. Resourceful companies, and people analyze their failures, extract valuable lessons, and bounce back stronger. This resilience transforms potential losses into valuable experiences that propel a company forward.

The Role of Leadership

Leadership plays a pivotal role in setting the tone for a culture of resourcefulness. Leaders who are themselves resourceful inspire the same trait in their teams by setting an example and rewarding innovative thinking and problem-solving.

Conclusion

The maxim "A company's greatest resource is resourcefulness" effectively encapsulates the essence of what propels a business to success in the contemporary commercial arena. While financial, technical, and material assets are essential, it is the intangible quality of resourcefulness that gives a company its competitive edge, fosters continuous improvement, and ultimately determines its longevity and prosperity. Undoubtedly, the ability to innovatively navigate the unpredictable currents of the business world stands as the hallmark of any truly thriving company.

ABOUT THE **AUTHOR**

Michael Gatewood has been serving in a leadership role for 30 years. He has served as a corporate trainer in south Florida for seven years. He has served as a Literature Evangelist, Team Leader, Unit Manager, Youth Care Worker III Group Supervisor, General Manager, Executive Coach and Bishop. My favorite thing in life is service. Leadership is not about giving orders as it is to fulfill what is ordered, Leadership is about being firm, fair and equitable. "as a Servant Leader I AM called by many, called out by one to serve those willing to accept service" Bishop Gatewood